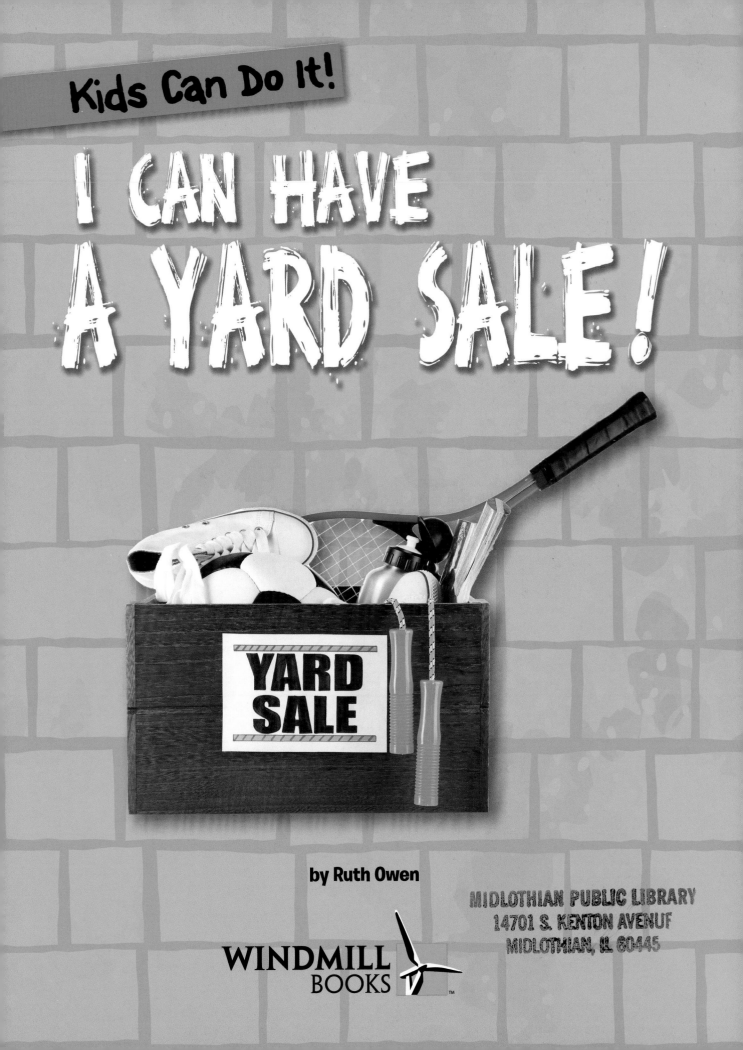

Kids Can Do It!

I CAN HAVE A YARD SALE!

by Ruth Owen

WINDMILL BOOKS ™

Published in 2018 by **Windmill Books**, an Imprint of Rosen Publishing
29 East 21st Street, New York, NY 10010

Produced for Rosen by Ruby Tuesday Books Ltd
Designer: Emma Randall

Photo Credits: Courtesy of Ruby Tuesday Books and Shutterstock.

Cataloging-in-Publication Data
Names: Owen, Ruth.
Title: I can have a yard sale! / Ruth Owen.
Description: New York : Windmill Books, 2018. | Series: Kids can do it! | Includes index.
Identifiers: ISBN 9781499483529 (pbk.) | ISBN 9781499483468 (library bound) |
   ISBN 9781499483352 (6 pack)
Subjects: LCSH: Garage sales--Juvenile literature. | Young businesspeople--Juvenile literature. |
   Entrepreneurship--Juvenile literature.
Classification: LCC HF5482.3 094 2018 | DDC 381'.195--dc23

Manufactured in the United States of America
CPSIA Compliance Information: Batch BS17WM: For Further Information contact Rosen Publishing, New York, New York at 1-800-237-9932

WARNING:

Some of the activities in this book require adult help.
It's also important that all laws and regulations are followed when
carrying out the activities in this book. The author and publisher disclaim
any liability in connection with the use of the information in this book.

CONTENTS

CASH FOR CLUTTER

Is the space beneath your bed bursting with old toys, books, and other junk you no longer need? Is it getting more and more difficult to close your closet doors?

Perhaps you're saving for a new laptop or skateboard, and it's taking forever? Or maybe you'd like to help out your favorite **charity** by making a **donation**?

If the answer is yes to any of those questions, then the solution to your problem could be to hold a yard sale. Not only will you clear some clutter, but you'll also make some cash!

What Is a Yard Sale?

A yard sale is an event organized in a yard or driveway. The people holding the sale sell off **secondhand** items they no longer need at low prices. Visitors to the sale get to buy objects at much cheaper prices than in a store.

REUSE, RECYCLE, REDUCE

Selling off the things you no longer want is actually really good for the planet.

Reuse

If you throw out these shoes that no longer fit, they will just end up in **landfill**. If you sell them at a yard sale, however, they will be reused by someone else!

Recycle

Many people like to craft and recycle unwanted objects into new things. A yard sale customer might buy your sweater . . .

. . . and recycle it into a cute cushion.

Reduce

Items that we buy from stores are often surrounded by packaging.

New toy with packaging   Secondhand toy

When customers shop at a yard sale, the items they buy are not encased in plastic or cardboard. This reduces the amount of packaging that needs to be produced and thrown away.

GET ORGANIZED!

Holding a yard sale is great fun, but it's also hard work. In order for your sale to be successful, you must get organized. So begin your preparations at least four to six weeks in advance.

1 The first thing to decide is where to hold your sale.

☆ Does your home have a driveway or large front yard where the sale can take place?

☆ Does your home have plenty of traffic and pedestrians passing by?

☆ Is there space on the street for several cars to park while customers visit your sale? Remember, you don't want them to park on your neighbors' property!

If the answer is no, ask a friend or family member if you can hold the sale in their driveway or yard.

2 Choose a date for your sale. If possible, avoid very cold or very hot times of the year, as the sale will be held outdoors. Weekends work best!

SEPTEMBER 2017

S	M	T	W	T	F	S
					1	2
3	4	5	6	7	8	9
10	11	12	13	14	15	16
17	18	19	20	21	22	(23)
24	25	26	27	28	29	30

This driveway is perfect for a yard sale. And if it rains, the sale could be held in the garage.

3 Ask some friends or family members to help with your sale. There's going to be lots to do before the sale and on the day of the sale. So having plenty of help makes good sense.

IT'S ALL ABOUT TEAMWORK

Ask an adult to help you contact your local government offices to find out if you need a **permit** to hold a sale. There may be a small charge for the permit. Also, ask if there are any **regulations** about putting up signs on the street to advertise your sale. Make sure you know the rules and then follow them!

COME TO A YARD SALE!

To have a successful yard sale, you will need plenty of customers. Therefore it's essential that you advertise your sale in advance and on the day of the sale.

1 Make posters to promote your sale. Make sure that the adult helping you is happy with the information you've included on your posters.

You can create one poster using markers and art supplies, then make copies. Alternatively, you can design your poster on the computer and then print out as many copies as you need.

YARD SALE

September 23rd
9:00 A.M. to 3:00 P.M.
2210 Maple Avenue

• Toys • Books • Video Games
• Knickknacks • Clothes
• Sports Equipment

YARD SALE

September 23rd
9:00 a.m. to 3:00 p.m.
2210 Maple Avenue

• Toys • Books • Video Games
• Knickknacks • Clothes
• Sports Equipment

You can print your posters onto brightly colored paper.

Display your poster in windows or on bulletin boards in places such as your school, local fitness center, community center, grocery store, or other places of business. Always ask permission before putting up a poster.

2 Go leafleting door-to-door. Make small versions of your poster and then deliver them to homes around your neighborhood during the week before your sale.

You can fit six leaflets on one sheet of printer paper.

Print out or make lots of copies.

Always go leafleting with a friend or an adult.

3 Tell everyone you know about your yard sale. Ask friends and family members to tell their friends and promote your sale on social media.

IT'S ALL ABOUT TEAMWORK

It's possible to promote your sale online. Many towns have community websites or Facebook pages where events such as yard sales can be advertised. With an adult, go online and check out all the opportunities for promoting your big day. Some towns or cities also have newsletters or free newspapers where you can advertise your sale.

4 On the day of your sale you'll want to direct people to your home. You can do this by making signs to put up around your neighborhood.

Figure out how many signs you'll need to make in advance.

Position signs at major intersections and on every turn that leads to your home.

You can use string to tie your signs to utility poles and trees.

5 Keep your street signs simple:

What are you promoting?

When is the sale?

What time is the sale?

Where is the sale?

YARD SALE

Saturday

9:00 a.m. to 3:00 p.m.

2210 Maple Avenue

6 Choose a color scheme, such as bright green, for your signs. Then customers will know to look out for the green signs.

YARD SALE →

SATURDAY 9 - 3

Have fun with your signs, but make sure they can easily be seen.

WHAT'S FOR SALE?

From the moment you decide to have a yard sale, start collecting **merchandise**.

Grab some old cartons and begin with your own bedroom. Check every drawer and closet and look under your bed. Anything you're happy to let go, put into a carton for your sale.

Ask the adults in your home if there are any items you can have for the yard sale.

If you have an attic or basement, ask if you can take a look for old toys and other salable items.

Tell all your friends and relatives what you're doing, and ask if they have anything they can donate to your sale.

Remember when you couldn't get to sleep without Mr. Dinosaur?

If he's now jammed at the back of your closet, maybe he's ready to be loved by a new owner. And he can earn you a few dollars!

Before putting an item into your box for sale, make sure you have permission to sell it.

Carefully check every item, too. For example, is there an important letter tucked inside an old book?

Could there be a forgotten $20 bill in the pocket of those jeans?

Do you have a huge box of Lego pieces you no longer want?

Buy some cheap paper lunch bags and tell customers they can fill a bag with Legos for a dollar.

Maybe you've collected lots of marbles, broken pieces of jewelry, or plastic beads left over from a crafting craze?

You can put these items into recycled glass jars. Customers will be happy to pay a few dollars for a jar of treasure!

FIXER-UPPERS

A broken item might still sell. It may be useful to someone who has the same item and needs spare parts.

Be honest with your customers. If something has a fault, write it on a label. Then the customer will know what they are buying and can make an informed decision.

Checkers

Includes:
Folding checkerboard
24 red and black
interlocking plastic checkers
Rules

For 2 players,
ages 6 to adult.

All playing pieces are in the box, but the rules and instructions are missing.

pressman

SELL REFRESHMENTS

Make iced tea and cookies to sell.

If your customers can buy a snack and a refreshing drink, they will stay longer at your sale **browsing** and buying.

Glass of iced tea and a cookie

$1

GET CREATIVE

Do you have old buttons, scraps of fabric, paper, or yarn? Fill clear plastic sandwich bags with these crafting scraps and sell them by the bag.

Flower Bouquet $1.50

Collect glass jars and recycle them as vases. Fill the jars with small bunches of flowers picked from your yard or the gardens of friends and family.

Always ask permission before picking flowers from a yard.

Many people who grow vegetables often have spare produce. Ask any gardeners you know if they can donate some excess veggies or fruit to your sale.

There's an old saying: *One person's trash is another person's treasure.*

Even if something looks hideous or is useless to you, DON'T assume someone else won't want it. In fact, it may be the first thing to sell!

GET THE PRICE RIGHT

In the weeks or days before your sale, mark each item with its price. This task is a lot of work, but it's worth it.

Customers browsing at a sale

Some people don't like having to ask for prices. These customers may visit your sale but leave without making a purchase if your merchandise isn't marked.

If your sale gets busy, having all the items priced means customers won't have to wait to speak to you. They will know instantly if the price is right for them.

If you're selling big items, use big price labels for easy visibility.

Be realistic when pricing secondhand goods. If an item costs $50.00 when new, a customer won't pay $40.00 for a battered, secondhand version!

$40.00 ✗

$5.00 ✓

Remember! You don't want these items. It's better to get a small amount of money for them than nothing at all.

 25¢   75¢  $1 $5

Use round numbers for your prices to make adding up quick and easy.

If you price your items in multiples of 25 cents, the only change you'll need will be quarters and dollars.

GET READY TO BARGAIN!

If you've priced an item at $5.00 a customer may offer $2.50. If you feel comfortable bargaining, your conversation might go like this:

You: I could drop the price to $4.00.
Customer: How about $3.00?
You: I'll take $3.50, but that's as low as I can go.

Bargaining is fun, but if you don't feel it's for you, that's fine. Just tell the customer that the original $5.00 price is final.

You can buy sticker price labels online or from stationery stores.

If you're sharing a yard sale with friends or family members, each pick a color and price your items with those labels. Then when a customer pays for an item you'll know who it belonged to.

Keep a record of each item that sells in a notebook.

Divide the pages of a notebook into columns for each seller.

Record each sale in the seller's column.

Sam	Alex	Mom	Sam	Alex	Mom
25¢	25¢	$5.00			
$1.00	50¢	$5.00			
$2.50	50¢	$10			
	25¢				
	25¢				
	$1				

At the end of the sale, you can add up the totals for each seller and divide up the money.

To keep things simple, you can give groups of items a single price. For example, all books are 25 cents each, or all DVDs are $1.00.

25¢ per book
5 books
for $1

Remember! You can do deals to encourage customers to buy more items.

Attract people to a table of merchandise with a big sign.

Make sure you still price the items individually, though, so that you and your helpers know how much to charge for the object.

Everything on this table $2.00

If you have lots of small toys to sell, try putting a collection into a clear plastic bag. Then sell the bag for 50¢ or a dollar.

If you have the instructions or original box for an item, you can usually charge a little more.

TAKE CARE OF THE DETAILS

You've advertised your sale, gathered your merchandise, and figured out your prices. Now the day of your yard sale is nearly here, so it's time to make some final preparations.

Clean up the yard, mow the grass, and if you have a pet dog, pick up any poop.

Make sure that any items that aren't for sale are packed away. You don't want one of your helpers accidentally selling Dad's new lawnmower for $10!

IT'S ALL ABOUT TEAMWORK

Be sure you have arranged to have at least one adult present to help out at your yard sale. It's your big day, but it is very important to have grown-ups around for your safety and in case you need their help or advice. It's especially important if you don't want to bargain on prices!

GET THE MOST FROM YOUR MERCHANDISE

Make sure that all your merchandise is clean. If any item is dusty or grimy, give it a polish or wipe it over with a damp cloth.

A pair of shoes won't be attractive to a customer if they're muddy.

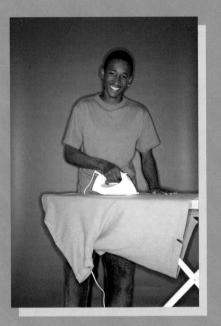

Pump up soccer balls and basketballs so customers know they are not damaged.

If items of clothing are rumpled, iron them.

If an item requires batteries, put some in so your customers can check that the item works.

In addition to your merchandise, you'll need packing material, change, and ways to display the items for sale.

If you're selling clothes, ask if anyone has a clothes rack you can borrow. Ask friends and family if they can donate some wire or plastic coat hangers, too.

You'll need tables to display your merchandise. Picnic tables or folding tables are perfect. You can cover them with a tablecloth or old white sheet to help make your displays look more attractive.

Your customers will enjoy browsing more if they don't have to bend too far to see what's for sale.

Collect plastic bags and small boxes so you can bag or pack your customers' purchases.

Collect as many old newspapers as possible for wrapping and protecting delicate items.

Add up your customers' purchases in your head if you can. Have a calculator ready as backup, however, just in case things get very busy and you need some help.

IT'S ALL ABOUT TEAMWORK

Ask an adult to help you organize plenty of spare change for the day of your sale. A good amount would be $50.00 made up of the following coins and bills.

$20 in quarters

10 × $1 bill

4 × $5 bills

THE BIG DAY!

The day of your yard sale has arrived. Put up the signs you made around your neighborhood very early in the morning or even the night before.

Allow plenty of time to display your merchandise. While some buyers like to rummage, most people quickly get tired of digging through dusty boxes. So display all the items you've collected in a way that makes them look great.

This may only be your yard or driveway, but for one day think of it as a shop filled with interesting treasures for sale!

Make sure each item and its price can easily be seen.

A cute display of toys for sale.

Display books or DVDs in a way that allows customers to see the front covers or spines.

Get creative and place items on your tables in themed groups.
Think about the stores you like best: How do they display their merchandise?

Sports equipment

Clothes and accessories

If customers are enjoying browsing, they will stay longer. If people passing by spot a crowd, they will be intrigued and want to take a look, too.

There's another old saying: *Nothing attracts a crowd, like a crowd.* If your yard sale display can attract a crowd, you'll make more money!

As customers arrive, welcome them by saying, "Hi" and giving them a smile.

Keep watch in case a customer has a question, but don't hover near people as this will make them feel uncomfortable!

Set up a pay station table that's close to the street. New visitors can easily ask you questions as they arrive, and people won't be able to leave without paying.

IT'S ALL ABOUT TEAMWORK

Be sure that you are ready to start your sale at the exact time you advertise. You may get some "early bird" customers who arrive before the sale starts. These buyers may be **dealers** who are looking for **antiques** or valuable items to sell in their shops. Ask your adult helpers to tell any early bird customers that they cannot buy anything until the sale officially opens.

If you're not selling food or drink, you can still offer your customers some free refreshment. Put out jugs of ice water for your visitors.

Remember! Keep your spare change and the money you take safe. Wear a fanny pack or apron with pockets.

Every now and then, put some of the money you've earned in a safe place inside the house.

When someone hands you a large bill, leave it in full view as you make their change. Then no one will be able to say that they gave you a $20 bill, when they only gave you $10!

As your merchandise begins to sell, keep moving items around to make your tables look as full as possible.

Remember, everything must go! So once your sale is half over, begin lowering your prices. Make some signs to let your customers know there are still lots of bargains.

Everything Must Go! All Items Half Marked Price

50% Off All Prices

Buy 1 Item Get a Second Item Free!

(The lowest priced item will be free.)

Alternatively, as customers arrive, give them a bag or a box and tell them they can fill it for $1.00.

Finally, it's closing up time. Pack up any leftover items in cartons ready to be donated to a charity. Clean up the yard and take down all the signs around your neighborhood.

Now it's time to count the cash. Add up the sales made by each seller and divide up the money. If you borrowed the $50 spare change from an adult, make sure you pay that back, too.

It's been a great day. You've recycled unwanted junk, donated some items to good causes, and made some cash.

Was it worth all the hard work? You bet!

antiques
Objects, such as pieces of furniture, paintings, or ornaments, that have a high value because they are old, high quality, or rare.

browsing
Looking at merchandise in a slow and casual way, with no rush to buy.

charity
An organization that raises money, often from donations, and then uses the money to help the needy or for other good causes.

dealers
People who buy and sell antiques.

donation
Something that is given for free; also a sum of money given to a charity or other cause.

landfill
Large sites where garbage is dumped and buried.

merchandise
Items for sale.

permit
An official document that gives someone permission to do something.

regulations
Rules that are made and enforced by a person or group in authority, such as local government.

secondhand
Something not new that was once used or owned by another person.

For web resources related to the subject of this book, go to:
www.windmillbooks.com/weblinks and select this book's title.

INDEX